Finding Mental Balance

Simple Practices for Managing Stress, Thoughts, and Emotions

compiled by KG Finfrock

This book is for informational and educational purposes only. It is not intended as medical, psychological, or professional advice. The reader assumes full responsibility for how the information is used.

ISBN: 979-8-9919775-1-7 (Paperback)
First edition

Published by Shrike Wire Press

Printed in the United States of America

Dedicated to my grandchildren.

May you always trust your inner voice and
treat yourselves with kindness.
May you grow into your strengths without
hardening your heart.
May you learn that calm is a form of courage,
and gentleness is never weakness.

Before You Begin

Mental balance isn't something we achieve once and then hold onto permanently. It's something we return to, especially during difficult moments. Stress and anxiety are part of being human, not signs that something is wrong with you. The practices in this book are meant to help you meet those moments with a little more steadiness, clarity, and kindness toward yourself.

The thoughts and reflections in this book are not offered as new or original ideas. They come from wisdom that has been shared, tested, and carried forward by many generations, across cultures and time. These are ways of understanding the mind and heart that people have returned to again and again, especially during moments of stress, anxiety, and uncertainty.

This book has no page numbers. There are no headers or titles (maybe a few). This book is not meant to be read in a straight line—though you're welcome to read it that way if it suits you. It was written to be opened wherever you are. You might begin at the beginning, somewhere in the middle, or by letting the pages fall open on their own. There is no correct order here—only what may be helpful in your current moment.

I've gathered these ideas and shaped them into simple language for everyday life, but their roots are much older than any one voice. They have endured because they continue to help people feel steadier, less alone, and more capable of meeting life as it is. They are included here because they still matter and because they bear repeating.

Each page offers a simple practice or way of thinking meant to support you through common mental and emotional challenges, such as stress that won't let up, anxious thoughts that repeat themselves, being emotionaly overwhelmed, self-criticism beating you down, uncertainty, or exhaustion.

Some pages may feel as if they speak directly to what you're facing; others may not resonate yet—and that's okay. You don't need to absorb everything or apply every idea. Take what helps, and leave behind what doesn't.

My hope is that when you open this book—whether intentionally or at random—you find something that meets you where you are. A thought that helps slow your racing mind. A reminder that eases tension, even slightly. A way to respond rather than react. If one page helps you feel more grounded or less alone in what you're carrying, then this book has done its work.

It's a new Dawn

It's a new Day

It's a new life for me

Lyrics from "Feeling Good" by Anthony Newley and Leslie Bricusse.

Don't Go Backwards.

Life feels lighter when you stop struggling against what cannot be controlled.

The rain will fall whether you complain about it or not.

Traffic will exist whether you stress or not.

People will act as they choose whether you worry or not.

Put your energy toward what you can influence.

Release what is not yours to carry.

Healing is your responsibility.
Growth is your decision.

It's a personal choice to live the way you do.

After a certain age, you are no longer the product of your environment or how you were raised. It's a personal choice to live the way you do. At some point, blaming your past becomes a distraction from your future.

Either take ownership of your life or become a prisoner to excuses.

Claim your freedom.
Self control is strength.
Calmness is mastery.

Let your mood rest on something sturdier than the passing actions of others.

Don't allow others to control the direction of your life.

Don't allow your emotions to overpower your intelligence.

Your peace grows when you stop letting small things others do determine how you feel.

Observe. Don't Absorb.

Not everything around you deserves to enter your mind.

A person's behavior is a reflection of their inner world — their fears, their wounds, their experiences. It's about them, not you.

Protect your inner environment like sacred ground.

Stay calm. Stay aware. Stay centered.

Observe the behavior. Learn from it. Do not carry it within you.

When you absorb negativity, you let others control your peace.

When you only observe, you stay in control of your energy.

The moment you stop internalizing what others do, you reclaim your power and protect your peace.

If words control you…
Everyone and anyone can control you.

You will continue to suffer if you have an emotional reaction to everything that is said to you.

True power is sitting back and observing everything with logic.

Treat someone as an option, and you'll be treated the same.

Cheat on someone, and betrayal will find you. Hurt others intentionally and pain will return to you.

Be rude without reason, and rudeness will meet you.

Use others for your needs, and you'll be used in turn.

When you act with sincere kindness, goodness has a way of returning. Life reflects what you put into it.

Power isn't in proving. It's in knowing you don't need to.

When they insult - stay silent, but smile.

When they lie - let truth unfold on its own.

When they shout - lower your tone.

When they blame - don't defend, just observe.

Tiny joys aren't so tiny.

Fresh Sheets.
A long shower.
Real belly laughs.
Someone checking in.
A song you forgot you liked.
Letting go of what that used to hold you back.
Finishing something you've been putting off.
A deep breath that actually feels relieving.
Sunlight coming from a window just right.
The quiet of a morning sunrise.

Pain is part of growing.

Everything in life is temporary.

Worrying and complaining changes nothing.

Every little struggle is a step forward.

Your scars are symbols of your strength.

What's meant to be will eventually be.

The best thing you can do is keep going.

Your entire life can change in a year. Your entire life can change in a moment.

Stop worrying about the big stuff because that's what paralyzes you.

Focus on getting the little things right every day and the positive ripple effect will be what changes your life.

When you detach from everything,
you attract everything.

When you no longer rely on external
validation to feel whole,
life naturally gravitates toward you.

When you stop needing anything to feel
complete, you begin gaining everything.

The most beautiful things arrive the moment
you stop chasing and allowing them in.

Know your truth.

Never say more than necessary.

Don’t allow your emotions to overpower your intelligence.

Lower your expectations from others.

Let your success do the talking.

10 people, 18 different opinions.

Stop trying to please everyone.

Don’t aspire to be perfect.

Don’t be afraid to say no.

Before you argue with someone, ask yourself, is that person mentally mature enough to grasp the concept of different perspectives.

If the answer is no, there's no point in continuing the discussion.

Don’t sit around hoping for change.

Get up.

Change your habits.

Smile often. Bring energy into your days.

Try things you’ve never done.

Clear out what weighs you down.

Unfollow people who drain your mind.

Sleep early. Rise early. Move with purpose.

Avoid gossip. Practice gratitude often.

Choose the things that strengthen you.

Be Bold.

You think disrespect is an insult. It is not.

Disrespect is information.

It tells you the person in front of you has low character, poor judgement, or deep insecurity.

It tells you they are not your people.

It tells you that you must move on.

Walk more, sit less—movement keeps life flowing.

Eat until you're 80% full—not stuffed.

Sleep like it's medicine—because it truly is.

Stay curious—a learning mind never grows old.

Protect your peace—drama kills quicker than disease.

Choose real food over packaged comfort.

Drink water like it's your daily ritual.

Keep good company—loneliness shortens life.

Forgive fast—bitterness poisons quietly.

Stay active—even a simple daily walk adds years.

Get sunlight—nature's free antidepressant.
keep your purpose alive—those without one fade early.

You arrive with nothing, spend your whole life chasing everything, and still depart with nothing. Fill your soul more than your hands.

The kindness you give out does not disappear. Even if it feels unnoticed or unreturned, your softness makes the world a little lighter. You never know who needs your patience, your smile, or your gentle words.

Keep showing the love.

You're planting seeds that will bloom in ways you may never fully see.

Become impossible to offend.
Let criticism bounce off, insults slide past, and let negativity flow through.

The person who can't be rattled can't be controlled.

The difference between a good day and a bad day is your attitude.

Your mind is a powerful thing.

When you fill it with positive thoughts, your life will start to change.

Consciousness is the state of being aware of and responsive to one's surroundings.

To shift your life, you must first shift your mindset.

Believe you can and you're halfway there.

Life becomes lighter the moment you stop gripping everything so tightly.

Let go of what you cannot control.
Let go of what is already gone.

Let go of the stories in your mind.

The more you loosen your hold, the more peace flows in.

Freedom doesn't come from having more.
Freedom comes from holding less.

When everything feels too big, go little. Wrap yourself with grace and space. Nibble your to-do's. Just one tiny bite at a time.

If you want to get more done, do less.

Stress dissipates in the face of guilt-free, intentional rest.

Nurture your friends.

Do not use them to solely unload your troubles and drama on their shoulders.

Balance what you feed them.

Don't make it all about you.

They can only carry so much weight before you overburden and overwhelm them.

Recognize when someone's outburst or attack is not about you.

Everyone has burdens and trauma that you are unaware of.

Freedom from debt is one less burden to carry.

Avoid debt whenever possible.

If you must borrow, borrow less and pay it off quickly.

Buy used instead of new when the function is the same.

An item is not on sale if you end up paying interest.

Interest is not savings—it is an added cost.

Tips to be Mentally Strong

Stop your expectations of others, focus on yourself.

Accept that life isn't always fair.

Don't beg for love or attention.

Keep your emotions under control.

Stay calm in the midst of chaos.

Don't take things personally.

Walk away from toxic people.

Focus on solutions, not problems.

Believe in yourself, always.

Practice these habits daily.

Anxiety isn't just fear. Anxiety is the mind's struggle with uncertainty.

When you can't tolerate the unknown, you try to control it through overthinking, overplanning, and overdoing. These actions only convinces your brain you're unsafe.

Let the uncertainty exist without fighting it.

When anxiety arises, notice when your body tightens around the unknown. Slow your breath and repeat, "I don't know what will happen. I am safe right now."

Do Not Poison Your Mind by these action

because …

Complaining only focuses on problems, not solutions.

Gossiping spreads negativity and weakens trust.

Envying destroys peace through comparison.

Comparing steals joy from your journey.

Consuming empties soul, never feels enough.

Doubting blocks growth and inner confidence.

Fearing limits potential and courage.

Hating poisons the heart, blinding you to

love.

Placing your hand on your heart while taking five deep breaths activates your parasympathetic nervous system and releases oxytocin.

This gentle self-touch tells your brain that you are safe and loved.

Suffering comes from trying to control what was never ours to control.
Look closely.
There are two worlds we live in every day:
What we can control and what we can't.
Most people exhaust their energy fighting the second one.

What IS in your control:
Your beliefs.
Your mindset.
Your attitude.
Your routines.
Your attention.
Your reactions.
Your boundaries.
Your relationships.
How you treat others.
How you spend your time.
How you talk to yourself.
This is your true power.

This is where change actually happens. When you choose patience over anger, discipline over excuses, kindness over ego —you are shaping your life from the inside out.

What is NOT in your control:
Other people's behavior.
Other people's beliefs and opinions.
Their words.
The past.
The future.
Weather.
Traffic.
Aging.
Uncertainty.
Natural events.
No amount of worry, overthinking, or emotional exhaustion will bend these to your will. Yet we give them our peace every day.

The moment you stop arguing with reality, you reclaim your calm. You don't need to control the world to be at peace. You only need to master your response to it.

> Focus where your power lives.
> Release what was never yours.
> Protect your energy like it's sacred —
> because it is.

Peace begins the day you stop trying to control everything and start taking responsibility for your inner world.

Your words shape your reality.

Choose words that help you cope, heal, and move forward—especially during difficult moments. Notice how you talk to yourself.

Don't speak words that reinforce hopelessness, shame, or defeat.

Intentionally use words that encourage steadiness, possibility, and self-respect. It doesn't mean pretending everything is fine or denying real struggles. It means not adding extra harm through harsh self-talk.

Replace "I can't handle this" with "This is hard, and I'm doing my best." Say "I'm learning" instead of "I always mess up."

Remind yourself that this feeling will pass when emotions feel overwhelming. Stop saying, "I'm tired. I'm broke. I'm depressed."

Start saying, "I'm grateful. I'm growing. I'm thriving."

What's good for your body is good for you.

Daily Walking - Heart
Proper Sleep - Brain
Sunlight exposure - Bones
Deep breathing - Lungs
Regular screen breaks - Eyes
Time with Loved Ones - Emotional health
Consistent sleep schedule - Body clock
Plenty of water - Kidneys
Garlic in meals - Boosts immune system

Things that seem like love:

- Physical intimacy
- constant phone calls
- obsession/attention
- frequent dates/gifts

What Love Truly Is:

- Trust
- Respect
- Sacrifice
- Forgiveness
- Commitment
- Shared goals
- Mutual support
- Growing together

When you can't calm your mind, calm your space.

Tidy a corner. Clear the sink. Light a candle. Start with what you can touch.

Sometimes order and repetitive movement can break the grip of mental chaos.

To attract better, you have to become better. You can't do the same things and expect change.

Transform your mindset.

Upgrade your habits.

Think positive.

Be hopeful and consistent with your evolution.

It all starts with you and how you feel about yourself.

Over time, priorities shift. What once felt exciting or tolerable begins to feel draining. You start to notice how certain environments, conversations, and relationships affect your energy and mood. This awareness isn't about becoming rigid or closed off—it's about learning what helps you feel steady and what doesn't. With that clarity, choices become simpler.

The older you get, the more you choose calm over chaos. You choose distance over disrespect. Drama becomes intolerable to you, and your peace becomes your ultimate priority. You start surrounding yourself with people who are good for your mental health, heart, and soul.

Your job is to stay rooted in who you are, act with integrity, stay devoted to your evolution, and let go of everything that isn't yours to carry.

Your job isn't to control how others think, act, or feel.

Happiness is not found, it's created through small daily choices.

Control your tongue, and you control half your problems.

Don't cling to things.

Desire is a cage that looks like freedom.

The quieter you become, the more you hear.

True wealth is measured in peace, not in gold.

Anger burns the one who holds it, not the one it's thrown at.

Ships don’t sink because of the water around them; ships sink because of the water that gets in them.

Don’t let what’s happening around you get inside you and weigh you down.

Attachment often turns into expectation. Expectation easily becomes disappointment. Disappointment brings pain.

The tighter we hold, the more we tend to suffer.

Everything in life is temporary—people, emotions, and moments all change. When we attach too tightly, we resist that change. That resistance is where much of our suffering begins.

The more your happiness depends on things staying the same, the more fragile it becomes. Then a single change, rejection, or ending can feel like it shakes everything.

Relief doesn't come from holding tighter. It comes from learning to hold with openness—allowing life to move while staying grounded within yourself.

If you wait until you feel better to start living, you might be waiting forever.

Go live your life.

Do it when sad. Do it when anxious. Do it when uncertain. Because healing doesn't always come before the experience.

Sometimes, the experience is what heals you.

Observations of Human Nature

Jealousy comes in jokes. Pay attention.

They want to see you do good,
but never better than them.

The longer the explanation, the bigger the lie.

A warrior's greatest weapon is patience.

A cat that dreams of becoming a lion
must lose its appetite for rats.

Some people are not your friends. They are
just scared to be your enemy.

If you do too much for people, they start
loving your hand and not your heart.

Not everyone you lose is a loss.
Some exits are blessings in disguise.

Most people don't want the truth.
They want comfort disguised as honesty.

Noticing these things isn't about becoming guarded—it's about moving through life with clarity and steadiness.

When we cling to pleasure,
we suffer when it changes.
When we resist pain, we suffer twice.
Wisdom comes from seeing clearly,
without attachment or aversion.

Do not chase happiness or fight suffering.

Observe to understand and to let go.

If it drains you, it is not for you.
Love, friendships, jobs, anything meant for you will nourish you, not exhaust you.

If you constantly feel depleted after being around someone or something, it is not aligned with your soul.

Your peace is the biggest sign of what belongs in your life.

Protect your peace.

Stop clinging to anger, regrets, and illusions of control. Every grudge you hold is a chain around your own heart.

The universe moves on whether you do or not.

Freedom only comes when you finally release.

Your brain doesn't need more cheap dopamine. You need connection, sunshine, nature, rest, exercise, and good music.

Do not hurt others with what brings pain to you.

Treat others the way you want them to treat you.

Do not do to anyone what you dislike for yourself.

Live in balance, for we are all connected.

Happiness is a choice, not a result.

Nothing will make you happy until you choose to be happy.

No person will make you happy unless you decide to be happy.

Your happiness will not come to you.

It can only come from you.

Every minute you spend trying to change what's outside your control is a minute you don't devote to what's actually in your power.

You only get so many minutes. Fill them with actions that could truly make a difference.

In a world where everything moves fast —our thoughts, our emotions, our reactions — One of the greatest skills you can develop is the ability to pause.

Pause before judging.
You never know the full story.
A moment of patience can save you from a lifetime of misunderstanding.

Pause before assuming.
Most assumptions are created by fear, not facts. Clarity begins when imagination ends.

Pause before accusing.
Words spoken in anger cannot be taken back.
A pause gives you space to see the truth, not just your emotions.

Pause before reacting harshly. A harsh response can damage relationships,hurt someone's heart, and leave you with regret.

A pause gives wisdom time to speak.

The pause matters because it creates space—between impulse and intention, between chaos and clarity, between emotion and understanding.

Most regrets come from reacting too quickly. Wisdom grows from taking a moment to reflect.

Practice the pause.

The pause is a small moment that protects your peace, your relationships, and your integrity.

You will be free once you realize the cage is made of thoughts. Not walls. Not fate. Not even your past.

Love needs action.

Trust needs proof.

Apologies need change.

Respect needs consistency.

Growth needs discomfort.

Healing needs time.

Peace needs boundaries.

Success needs discipline.

Happiness needs gratitude.

Understanding needs listening.

Nothing lasts forever—the moment will pass.

Every struggle is a lesson in disguise.

Don't forget to laugh, even now.

You've faced storms before —you'll survive this one too.

Be gentle with yourself. Self-kindness heals the deepest wounds.

Don't carry the weight of people's negativity.

Sometimes not getting what you want is life protecting you.

There is always something to be grateful for—always.

You'll be alone in the most difficult times of your life.

These times will make you wise, mature, and fearless. They will strip away every illusion and show you who truly matters.
You'll learn to be your own strength when no one shows up.

In silence, you'll meet the strongest version of yourself.

Pain will become your greatest teacher, and growth will become your quiet reward.

One day, you'll look back and realize solitude was a blessing in disguise.

Truths That Support a Lasting Relationship

A partnership with someone doesn't fix your wounds. Heal yourself before you commit.

Love fades without respect. Respect must always come first.

Money secrets destroy marriages faster than infidelity.

Long-term stability comes from shared values.

Choose carefully who you share relationship challenges with. Too many voices can weaken trust.

Ego kills faster than mistakes. Learn to say sorry.

Silence calms your mind.
Long walks refresh your soul.

Time alone recharges your energy.
Let go of perfection and be real.

Laugh freely with good friends.

Appreciate how far you've come.
Spend time in nature and feel its peace.

Rest without guilt.

Choose kindness —
especially toward yourself.

Drinking warm water before meals boosts digestion and detoxifies your gut.

Sleeping before 11 PM heals your brain and balances hormones.

Walking for 30 minutes daily strengthens your heart, brain, and bones.

Sitting in the sun for 15 minutes increase your Vitamin D which strengthens immunity.

Eating slowly and chewing properly improves digestion and prevents overeating.

Eating one fruit on an empty stomach cleanses your system and energizes you.

Practice deep breathing for five minutes to reduces stress, anxiety, and blood pressure.

Respecting yourself begins with listening.

Your body asks for a break not to slow you down, but to keep you well.

Your mind seeks rest when it has carried too much.

Pausing allows clarity to return and tension to soften.

Needing space is not selfish or weak. It is how you protect your balance and inner peace. When you honor these needs without guilt, you practice true self-care—and from that care, strength quietly grows.

Speak positive words into your life every single morning.

Think big.

Think healing.

Think success.

Think peace.

Think happiness.

Think growth mindset.

Always start the day with positive energy.

Let them…

If they want to leave, let them.
If they choose someone else, let them.
If they don't support you, let them.
If they don't invite you, let them.

Stop wasting your energy
trying to control or change other people.

Let them show you who they really are.
And then choose what you do next.

If it still bothers you after 24 hours, speak up within 48 hours.

Treat yourself in the same manner you would take care of someone you loved and were responsible for their well being.

A bad day doesn't mean a bad life.

There's a difference between honest self-reflection and the destructive voice that tears you down. The harsh inner critic doesn't always tell the truth. Constructive reflection helps you grow.

Your brain can't be grateful and anxious at the same time. When anxiety takes hold, look for gratitude.

Stop apologizing for expressing your feelings. You're convincing yourself that you are not worth the space you take up.

- Wake up early.
- Make your bed.
- Enjoy the morning sun.
- Set intentions for your day.
- Speak kindly to yourself.
- Enjoy your coffee.
- Go on a walk without distractions.
- Talk to your friends and family.
- Learn something new.
- Fuel yourself with whole foods.
- Practice gratitude.
- Surround yourself with people who lift you up.

These small, steady choices create a life that feels balanced, supported, and well lived.

Smiling attracts positivity.

Quiet reflection attracts clarity.

Exercising attracts energy.

Learning attracts progress.

Staying calm attracts peace.

Setting goals attracts success.

Eating mindfully attracts vitality.

Your daily choices influence the energy, clarity, and direction you experience.

What you nurture within yourself begins to meet you in the world

Stop …

Overthinking everything.

Holding grudges for too long.

Comparing your life with others.

Staying in friendships that drain you.

Waiting for the perfect moment to start.

Saying yes when you want to say no.

Carrying guilt for things you cannot change.

Chasing people who do not value you.

Doubting your own abilities.

Keeping habits that make you unhappy.

Freedom begins when you stop carrying what no longer serves you.

You disrespect yourself when you beg someone for bare minimum things like:

- love
- attention
- support
- reciprocation

Do not disrepect yourself.

Never lower your standards to keep someone in your life.

Love and attention should be freely given, not earned through begging.

When you beg for basic things, you diminish your own sense of worth and self-respect.

Invest your energy in those who meet you halfway and appreciate you fully.

Respect yourself enough to walk away from anything that makes you question your value.

In today's world, it's easy to confuse intensity with intimacy…
attention with affection…
and obsession with love.

Many things look like love on the surface, but real love is much deeper, quieter, and stronger than momentary excitement.

Things That Seem Like Love

Physical intimacy: Closeness of the body doesn't always mean closeness of the heart.
Constant phone calls: Attention isn't the same as affection.
Obsession or over-possessiveness: This is insecurity dressed up as love.
Frequent dates and gifts: Beautiful gestures, but they don't build a relationship by themselves.
These things may feel good, but they can disappear just as quickly as they appear.

True Love Is …

Trust: The foundation of every unbreakable relationship.
Respect: Without this, love cannot survive.
Sacrifice: Choosing the relationship over convenience.
Forgiveness: Because both people will make mistakes.
Commitment: Staying when it's difficult, not just when it's easy.
Shared goals: Building in the same direction. Not pulling apart.
Mutual support: Being each other's safe place through storms and sunshine.
Growing together: Not staying the same, but evolving side by side.

Love is not loud.
Love is not needy.
Love is not controlling.

Real love is steady, patient, secure, and built on actions that last beyond the moment.

Don't settle for the illusion of love when you deserve the real thing.

Once you stop rushing through life,
you'll be amazed at how much more life you
have time for.

Practice the pause.
Pause before judging.
Pause before assuming.
Pause before accusing.

Pause whenever you're about to react harshly and you'll avoid doing and saying things you'll regret.

Silence doesn't always mean you have nothing to say. It may mean you realize that no matter what you say, it won't change anything.

Touching a tree—especially when standing barefoot on the ground—can literally change your state of mind.

In a world wired with screens and stress, our bodies are still built for nature.

Grounding, or "earthing," isn't just hippie talk—studies suggest it can calm your nervous system, steady your breath, and melt away stress.

Defeat is psychological.

Losing only becomes permanent when you believe it is. The truth is, as long as you're breathing, you still have time to pivot, rebuild, and rise. Pain is real, setbacks are real, but staying stuck is a decision.

The mind will try to convince you it's over. That you're not enough. That you should quit. But if you train your mind to see failure as feedback and pressure as preparation, you become unstoppable.

Winners lose just like everyone else.
They just refuse to stay there.

Control your mind and you control the outcome.

Learn to delay your reaction.

Anger, fear and impulse will make you move fast.

Power is in pausing.

Wisdom lives in the pause.

In the pause, you see clearly, you respond wisely, and you avoid decisions you'll regret.

Experience new things.

Love the people around you.

Eat nourishing food.

Live in the moment.

Focus on your passion.

Give back.

Listen to music.

Spend time in the sunshine.

Develop a desire to grow and evolve.

Make a difference where you can.

Move your body.

Quiet your mind.

I am in competition with no one.
I have no desire to play the game of being
better than anyone.
I am simply trying to be better than the
person I was yesterday.

Not every argument is worth your time.
Not every disagreement deserves your energy.
And not every person is capable of understanding a perspective that isn't their own.
Before you dive into an argument, take a moment to pause and reflect:
Is this person mentally mature enough to grasp different viewpoints? Because if someone lacks emotional intelligence, if they're driven by ego instead of understanding, if they hear only to reply and not to understand —then no amount of explanation will ever reach them.
You can't reason with someone who is committed to misunderstanding you.
You can't teach perspective to someone who only wants to be right.
You can't expect depth from someone who has never looked inward.

Arguments with such people drain your peace, waste your time, and leave you frustrated.
Meanwhile, silence protects your energy and preserves your dignity.
Choose your battles wisely.

Choose your peace wisely.

A wise person knows when to speak…
and when to walk away, because the listener is not ready.

Don't use your energy to worry.

Instead, use your energy to believe, to create, to trust, to grow, to glow, to manifest, and heal.

Your entire destiny follows where your energy flows.

Sometimes you need to unlove people to get back to yourself.

No matter what, you'll be judged, so do it anyway.

Regrets hurt more than failure; don't hold yourself back.

Your thoughts control you only if you let them.

You need to cut off toxic people to realize the value of your life.

Your circle gets narrower as you get older because you realize the importance of quality.

You cannot suffer in the past or future because they do not exist.

What you are suffering is your memory of the past or your imagination of the future.

A person's behavior is a mirror of their inner world. It's about them, not you.

Protect your inner environment like sacred ground.

Observe their behavior. Learn from it. Do not make it yours.

How do you let go of the past?
By realizing it no longer exists.

The past only lives in one place, in your mind. Not at this moment. Not in reality. Only in memory.

We don't suffer because the past is still happening. We suffer because we keep replaying it.

Steps Toward Mastering Your Emotions

Identify the Trigger. The fastest way to recalibrate is to notice what set you off. Analyze the pattern and energy beneath the surface and ask yourself, "What is this trigger showing me?"

Witness with Neutrality. Emotions lose their power when they are seen clearly. Instead of suppressing or amplifying them, sit as the observer. "I notice anger is here" is different from "I am angry".

Clear the static. Old emotional residue hides in your body and can look like a tight jaw, hunched shoulders, or tension that signals stagnant energy. Shake, stretch, move, and release it.

Rewrite the story. Every thought repeats a timeline. "This always happens" keeps you locked in replay. Shift to "I'm meeting this differently now." Write a new narrative intentionally.

Anchor the nervous system. Your body decides faster than your mind. Slow your heart rate, deepen your breath, and balance your posture. A calm system transforms any emotional hijack.

Return to the Now. Most emotional surges are past echoes or future fears. Bring yourself back into this single moment. Presence dissolves illusions and reveals what's truly here.

Create a Release. Don't let emotions calcify into your baseline. Journal, feel, and move them through. Expression clears the slate for clarity. Create closure, as suppression only breeds confusion.

Reinforce Action. Integration happens when you act from the state you want to anchor. If you want to embody calm, make one calm choice. If you want to embody strength, take one courageous step. Action is the loudest affirmation.

It is easy to forget how blessed we are. To wake up, to eat well, to move our bodies, to care for others. Even the tired moments mean we are alive.
Gratitude is found in the ordinary, and that is what makes life beautiful.

You become humble once you realize that
anything can happen; sickness, death, losing
your job, literally anything can disappear in
the blink of an eye.
Tables turn, and that's how crazy life can get.
Always stay connected to your higher self,
stay humble, and be thankful.

Things to Practice

1. Let it go.
When someone triggers you, pause and let it go. Triggers are not punishments — they are mirrors. They show you where healing is still needed. Release the need to react. Peace grows in non-reaction.

2. Accept what is.
Wishing reality was different only creates resistance and suffering. Acceptance is not giving up — it is grounding yourself in truth. Start where you are. Use what you have. Move forward from reality, not fantasy.

3. Let them.
If they want to leave, let them.
If they want to misunderstand you, let them.
If they want to be unhappy, let them.
Everyone is on their own journey. You don't need to manage other people's life lessons.

4. Trust in timing.
What is meant for you will arrive when you are ready — not when you are anxious. Delays are not denials. Life unfolds with intelligence. Trust the process, even when you don't see the full picture.

5. Look for glimmers.
Glimmers are the opposite of triggers. They are small moments of safety, joy, beauty, or calm — a smile, a quiet breath, sunlight, laughter. Train your mind to notice them. What you notice, grows.

It's about releasing what no longer serves you and living with more awareness, trust, and gentleness.

Practice these daily — and watch your life soften.

A Note From The Author

This is the section of the book where I tell you who I am, what I've accomplished, buy my other books, blah blah blah.

Here's the truth: none of that really matters. This book isn't about me. It's about you — your growth, your balance, and your life.

If you have picked it up, it means you are searching for answers. I hope you find them.

The words in this book are from ancient life teachings. Knowing these words and applying the words are two very different things.

We need to practice the words to build our inner strength and to do that, sometimes we need reminders. This book is the reminder. Keep the book visible.

If I were to narrow this book down to a few core lessons, they would be:
Pause to take a step back
Observe so you see a larger picture of what is happening and why it is happening.

Choose whether to engage or disengage. You don't have to take the bait a toxic person hands you.

Your path in life is a journey that you walk alone although many may share your experiences. Try not to presume you know them or judge them when you first meet. You will not know their current or past burdens or the trauma they carry. You may find yourself surprised.

Live long. Live with peace in your heart. Find and keep the calmness within you.

www.ingramcontent.com/pod-product-compliance
Lightning Source LLC
LaVergne TN
LVHW090532110826
845146LV00003B/1066

* 9 7 9 8 9 9 1 9 7 7 5 1 7 *